Play School Play Ideas 2

The continuing success of the original *Play School Play Ideas* has led to this second book. Here are hundreds more different ideas for play with the under-fives. There are things to make, games to play, and ideas for amusing children in and out of doors, and none of them needs expensive or specialised equipment. In fact, most of the ideas make use of everyday materials and packaging normally consigned to the dustbin.

Carole Ward has worked on *Play School* as both presenter and director. She has also written scripts for the programme and is a trained infant-school teacher.

Many a harassed parent will welcome this second permanent record [illegible]
Play School.

Play School Play Ideas 2

Carole Ward

Drawings by Quentin Blake

BBC/KNIGHT BOOKS

First published by the
British Broadcasting Corporation 1977

*This edition first published by the British Broadcasting Corporation/
Knight Books 1984*

British Library C.I.P.
Ward, Carole
Play school play ideas 2.
1. Infants 2. Amusements
I. Title II. British Broadcasting Corporation
649′.5 GV1203

ISBN 0 340 36387 8
0 563 20340 4 (BBC)

Printed and bound in Great Britain for the British
Broadcasting Corporation, 35 Marylebone High Street,
London W1M 4AA and Hodder and Stoughton
Paperbacks, a division of Hodder and Stoughton Ltd.,
Mill Road, Dunton Green, Sevenoaks, Kent (Editorial
Office: 47 Bedford Square, London, WC1 3DP) by
Richard Clay (The Chaucer Press) Ltd,
Bungay, Suffolk

Contents

Acknowledgements

William Collins Sons and Co. Ltd. for *Water*, JOHN CROSSLAND; Evans Bros for *Go Out*, EILEEN MATHIAS from "Fancy Free"; William Heinemann Ltd. for *Without any legs*, an extract from *Spells*, JAMES REEVES from "The Wandering Moon"; David Higham Associates Ltd. for *I hate this hat*, *My neck is amazingly endlessly long*, and *A pound of stones*, SHIRLEY GEE; Macmillan, London and Basingstoke, for *I can think sharply*, ALAN BROWNJOHN, and *Sink song*, J. A. LINDON from "Rhythm Rhyme Green Book"; The Estate of Ogden Nash for *Behold the duck*; *Hands are very handy things*, JEAN WATSON; Eileen Weaver for *How did the music of the world begin?* STEPHEN WEAVER; *The Chestnut trees are a market square*, PATRICIA ROPES; *What is pink?* and *Brown and furry*, CHRISTINA ROSSETTI; *Be kind and courteous*, *When daisies pied* and *You spotted snakes*, WILLIAM SHAKESPEARE from "A Midsummer Night's Dream"; *A bubble grows bigger and bigger*, *Creeping quietly through the jungle*, *Do you like to jump in puddles?* *Five small seeds*, *Flowers first, then petals fall*, *Fly fly fly butterfly*, *How many pips in an apple?* *I like to spin gigantic webs*, *It started right up here*, *Legs are very useful things*, *My fingers are grass*, *Octopus, octopus*, *On a beach what can you find?* *Once a man*, *Sea whisper*, *Stand in the sun*, *Two metal arms*, *What's inside an empty tin?* are © British Broadcasting Corporation 1977; the remainder of the verses are from traditional sources.

Introduction

Going out, trying out, finding out, sorting out and helping out, are activities and experiences common to any age, but this book highlights jobs, games, poems and rhymes which can be shared by adult and child. Also, there are ideas for making, inventing, chattering and storytelling, with suggestions for ways in which one may grow from the other.

As one of the first presenters of *Play School* and later a member of the production team, Carole Ward has wide experience of the technique of "speaking" directly to a child who may be watching the programme alone. But although this one to one relationship is the programme's first principle it is difficult to interpret it in a book for a child who cannot read. Therefore Carole Ward writes for anyone who is involved with young children and who needs more ideas for encouraging their play, their widening of experience and their help with everyday chores.

Quentin Blake's drawings sum up one of our constant dilemmas – how to offer ideas which will extend the child's experience and enjoyment while admitting that initial inability and excessive energy may produce a certain amount of chaos! We hope that some of our "clearing up" and "putting away" suggestions go some way to make amends!

Between 1964 and 1977, Nancy Quayle was our adviser. It was her advice, humorous anecdotes and information which reminded us of the vulnerability, delights and possibilities of the earlier years of childhood.

Cynthia Felgate

Sorting Out

If all the world were paper,
And all the sea were ink,
If all the trees were bread and cheese,
What should we have to drink?

An old box with a cellophane window standing on its side becomes a **fish tank**. Tiny paper fishes, seahorses and octopi, can be hung on cotton, through slits cut in the top, and made to swim up and down.

Make an **octopus** with four strands of wool doubled over and tied in a knot at the top.

Octopus, octopus,
Do you ever worry
About getting in a muddle
When swimming
In a hurry?

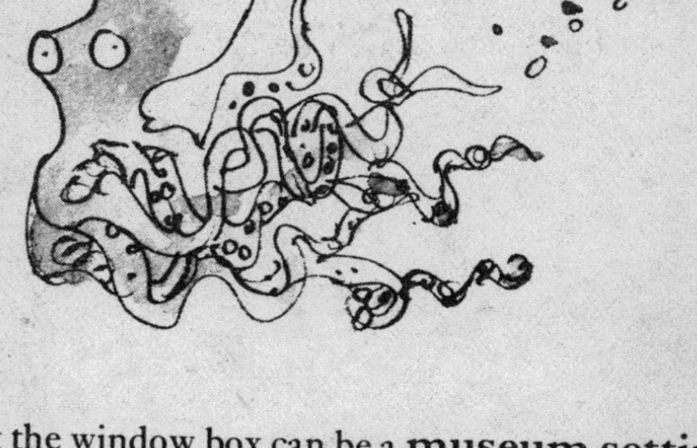

Laid flat the window box can be a **museum setting** for collections. Either stick the items down for keeps, or change them for special showings: stones, bones, stamps, old postcards, very small things, insects (dead), buttons, tiny glass bottles (these really might prove worth collecting!)

Polystyrene food trays can have items arranged on them. Or they can be made into **ready-framed pictures**. Paint something in the middle and hang with a piece of string.

One idea could be a **beach picture**. Use bits of old sandpaper for the beach. Scrumpled blue tissue makes an excellent wavy sea, and a little pulled out cotton wool has the sea breaking on the shore. Collections of small shells could be added.

Other uses for polystyrene trays: baby's play things, a guitar (stretch elastic bands of different thicknesses over the tray), roofs on houses or garages, disposable plates for picnics, cargo ships for bath, puddle or pool, moulds for plaster printing casts (see page 89).

Keep that old scrubbing brush even if it has only a few remaining bristles. Rubbed round and round on brown paper it makes a very realistic sea sound.

Sea whisper
Sea sound
Salt-tasting sea.
Sea swirl
Sand stir
Shell song sea.

Tightly rolled-up newspaper, the edges stuck with wall-paper paste, makes strong **building material** for tunnels, bridges, viaducts and spaghetti junctions. Bend them and tie them with string or elastic bands. Flat cardboard, stuck on, makes a road for toy cars.

Bend a long roll of newspaper for two legs. Secure a short thick roll for a body and one across for two arms and you have a **doll**. Draw or paint a face on a small paper bag. Stuff it with newspaper and add wool or paper twists for hair. Make rag or newspaper clothes.

In packaging you sometimes get thin layers of foam rubber. These could replace the newspaper rolls to make a doll.

For **paper twists** run thin strips of paper firmly between thumb and pencil. Newspaper is not so good for this, but old torn up envelopes will do.

Old envelopes can be: drawn on, used as markers, have things kept in them, become dolls' hats, long ones can be hand puppets for small hands, or just be used as envelopes for post people! Letters posted into an old tissue box can be collected any time!

Tissue boxes can be useful for storing things. If dropped, the contents are half held in! Collect different coloured boxes for identification.

Cut a long strip of old wall-paper about a foot deep. Paste pictures from old magazines or draw a **journey back cloth**: country scenes, animals, farms, woods, factories on the edge of town, houses, shops, police station, garages, flats, park, library, zoo, lakes, fields, a river, the sea. Use it as a memory roll. As you slowly unroll it what comes next? Hold it out at ground level against a wall or between two chairs. Traffic can ride along the floor in front of it. Using the same idea make up a story and pass the whole roll through a cellophane window box.

Keep cut-out pictures from old magazines in boxes. Sort into animals, people, flowers etc., and label each box with a cut-out.

If cutting out is difficult, see if pin pricking can help. With a large pin prick holes round the picture, keeping them close together. Then pull the picture away from the page.

See a pin and pick it up
And all the day you'll have good luck!

Make your own **sewing cards**. Find a picture with a clear outline; an umbrella, a flower, a car, stick it on to thin cardboard and prick large holes about $\frac{1}{2}$ cm apart, round the edge. Thread lengths of wool through a large bodkin, using a double thread so the needle won't come off or get lost. Weave the thread in and out of the holes.

Bring out cut-out pictures on a rainy day. Choose a few at random and test the best storyteller to make up a **story** using all the chosen pictures. Even more testing – hold up one picture at a time and ask the storyteller to incorporate the subject into his or her story. See how long you can keep the story going.

I'll tell you a story about Jackanory
And now my story's begun
I'll tell you another
About Jack and his brother
And now my story is done!

There are stories that never end!

One dark and stormy night when the waves were as big as houses and the clouds growled over the moon a group of sailors sat listening to tales of the sea.
"Tell us another," said the captain. A sailor began.
"One dark and stormy night when the waves were as big as houses and the clouds growled over the moon a group of sailors sat listening to tales of the sea.
'Tell us another,' said the captain. A sailor began. 'One dark and stormy night . . .' "

Who put the football through the window-pane?
Nobody answered so I said it once again.
Who put the football through the window-pane?
Nobody answered so I said it once again.
Who put the football through the window-pane?
Nobody answered so I said it once again.
Who put . . .

Pictures of single objects a child will recognise can become a **picture game**. Stick the pictures on to the backs of old writing pads or the cardboard from cut-up cereal packets. Hold up the pictures one at a time. The idea is to clap three times, then shout out what's on the card. Keep a rhythm going. It's more difficult than it seems!

When you are looking for pictures in magazines also look for plain coloured bits of paper, however small. If torn into pieces and kept until quite a quantity has been collected they can be made into **mosaic pictures** and patterns. Use a thin wall-paper paste for sticking. It leaves no marks on the finished work and is easily washed off surrounding areas!

What is pink? A rose is pink
By the fountain's brink.
What is red? A poppy's red
In its barley bed.
What is blue? The sky is blue
Where the clouds float thro'.
What is white? A swan is white,
Sailing in the light.
What is yellow? Pears are yellow,
Rich and ripe and mellow.
What is green? The grass is green,
With small flowers between.
What is violet? Clouds are violet
In the summer twilight.
What is orange? Why, an orange –
Just an orange!

Keep any small pieces of "see-through" coloured paper. They can be arranged on to the back of paper doilies and stuck down with tiny dabs of wall-paper paste. Then hang the **stained glass picture** against the light. You could cut your own holes out of paper making specific shapes. Bits of tissue paper stuck to the back would also let the light through.

Old scraps of tissue paper can be used for making flowers to put in miniature gardens.

A-tishoo! A-tishoo!
One for a wish
Two for a kiss
Three for a letter
Four for something better!

Make a large **greeting or birthday card** for someone you know well by finding pictures of all the things he or she likes. Arrange them as a montage overlapping one another.

Stick a picture on to a stiffish card. Cut round the top of the picture. Bend a bit back either side and you have a free-standing card. This idea could be used for **place names** at parties.

Old Christmas and birthday cards can be reused as **gift tags**. Choose suitable pictures (no fond messages on the back) and cut out to bell or candle shape. Blunt pinking shears (too blunt for material that is) make square shapes interesting.

Pictures can be stuck on cardboard and cut up to make **jigsaws**. Obviously the smaller you cut the more difficult they will be to put back together! A tip for home-made puzzles is to paint the backs with a wash of paint for future identification. Then store the pieces in individual bags or boxes and mark on them the number of pieces there should be for each. If they do get mixed up, a sorting game can be to put them back in the right bags or boxes.

A simple **paper hat** is a strip held together with two paper clips.
Corks or screwed-up bits of paper tied with string to the brim of an old hat keep the flies away from your face when sitting in the jungle or desert! If not, sing this song to the tune of "John Brown's Body" and do the actions.

I'm sitting in the jungle
When a fly sits on my nose,
Sitting in the jungle
When a fly sits on my nose,
Sitting in the jungle
When a fly sits on my nose,
So I flip it and I flop it
And the fly flies away.

I'm sitting in the desert
When a fly sits on my nose,
Sitting in the desert
When a fly sits on my nose,
Sitting in the desert
When a fly sits on my nose,
So I flip it and I flop it
And the fly flies away.

I'm sitting in the forest
When a fly sits on my nose,
Sitting in the forest
When a fly sits on my nose,
Sitting in the forest
When a fly sits on my nose,
So I flip and I flop it
And the fly flies away.

Make up different words to suit your own location!

For an instant **spider** tear off one section of a cardboard egg box. Tear eight slits in it and then press four pipe cleaners across the body into the slits. Bend the legs into a realistic shape.

I like to spin gigantic webs,
I bend and stretch my eight thin legs,
And twist and turn and wind the thread.
I'm a spider!

I like to curl up very small
To look like dust upon the wall,
But flies must watch out if they call.
I'm a spider!

And if you break my web, take care,
For I can travel through the air,
Upon my thread as fine as hair
I'm a spider!

A strip of corrugated paper can have feathers or grasses stuck in it for a **headdress**.

A **hat** for a small head or doll can be an old paper plate. Make two holes either side of the plate then thread wool or string through to tie. All sorts of things can decorate the top.

To make a **remembering game**, stick pictures of different objects, animals, etc., on to a tall paper hat. Allot the time that the player may look at the hat by the number of pictures: six pictures – a slow count of six, eight pictures – a slow count of eight. Then place the hat on the player's head. Now, what's on the hat?

I hate this hat,
It's so boring and plain.
I hate this hat,
Get a nice bath mat,
And put a cat on the top,
A ginger cat,
That's enormously fat.
Perhaps a flower would help – now stop.

This hat I hate,
Perhaps a roller skate
Would make it much finer,
And a small fish on a large dish
And a plastic ocean liner?
What about a light
To glow quite bright?
That will make my hat a winner
A white beehive and the number five,
And a plate with all my dinner!
How's that?

This hat I hate,
So off with the plate
And the number five
And the glowing light
And the white beehive
And the boat and the fish
And the skate and the dish
And the flower and the cat
That's enormously fat
And the old bath mat. . . .

I like this hat,
Right now, like this,
It's a good plain hat
Just as it is!
How's that?

The usual junk items, boxes, cartons, cardboard rolls, packaging, can be built into a **tower** for knocking over. Paper darts have to knock it down.

They can also make an **obstacle race** for your toys. Boxes to climb over. Cardboard rolls to go round. Cereal boxes to go through. A stick across two boxes as a high jump. Screwed-up newspaper gives them a safe landing!

Build a **block of flats** for a toy out of boxes from the supermarket.

I built (name of toy) *a block of flats,*
I built them in the city,
Put her in
But she jumped out
So fare ye well, my darling!

I built (name of toy) *a high brick wall,*
I built it in the garden,
Put him in
But he jumped out
So fare ye well, my darling!

Cardboard boxes stuck together make a realistic **robot**. Paint on knobs and dials.

Two metal arms
And two metal legs
Fixed to a body
With strong metal pegs.

A head on top
Like an old tin can
With two green eyes
It's a Robot Man!

One grey elephant balancing
Carefully on a piece of string,
Thought it such a wonderful stunt
He called for another elephant.

Two grey elephants balancing
Side by side on a piece of string,
Thought it such a wonderful stunt
They called for another elephant.

Three grey elephants balancing
Side by side on a piece of string,
Thought it such a wonderful stunt
They called for another elephant.

Four grey elephants balancing
Side by side on a piece of string,
Thought it such a wonderful stunt
They called for another elephant.

(When you want to end it . . .)

What do you think happened? –
All the elephants fell off!

Make a cardboard roll into a stand-up **mouse**. Tear or cut two slits opposite each other in the top of the roll and stick in two round pieces of card for ears. Cross and stick on two long thin pieces of paper for whiskers and crayon on the eyes and nose. Add string to the bottom for a tail.

By the same method make an **angel**. Put one big circle into the slits at the top, and crayon on a face. Cut out wings and stick on the back or wrap a paper doily round as a cloak. Draw on folded arms and hands.

Build a **pyramid** with cardboard rolls. Make two slits about half an inch apart in one side of the top of a roll. Repeat the opposite side and at the bottom. Do this to other rolls, now fit them all together. Corrugated paper or stiff cardboard with slits in can also be made into modern sculptures or versatile buildings.

String tied from a high level to a low can provide a **bush telegraph**. Send down tissue boxes, cardboard rolls, plastic containers, in which are picture clues for nursery rhymes: spider, pail of water, feather, lamb, roses in a ring.

A ring, a ring o' roses,
A pocket full of posies,
Ash-a! Ash-a!
All stand still.

The king has sent his daughter
To fetch a pail of water,
Ash-a! Ash-a!
All bow down.

The bird upon the steeple
Sits high above the people,
Ash-a! Ash-a!
All kneel down.

The wedding bells are ringing
The boys and girls are singing,
Ash-a! Ash-a!
All fall down.

Fold up a long thin strip of paper backwards and forwards into a concertina design. At one end draw two eyes and stick on a long thin tongue. Slither the **snake** along pulled by a piece of thread.

Make another zig-zag out of a strip of stiff paper and stick one end in a small box. Press it all down with the lid. When you open the lid? Out it pops!

Make a **pop-up game** from a cone of stiff paper, a stick, and two cardboard circles. The cone should have a hole at the bottom for the stick to move through, and the circles be small enough to disappear inside the cone. Colour the circles different colours then stick them back to back together to one end of the stick. Put the stick through the cone. Now, facing your audience, pop the circle up from inside the cone. Pop it down and turn the circle round inside the cone. Pop it up again. The audience sees a different colour! You can make your own "magic suspense" chat. Instead of colours, you could draw one sad and one happy face.

Very small cones stuck together with all the points facing inwards, make **balls** for decoration. Made out of old magazines they look very colourful. You need about twenty cones per ball and quite strong glue for the middle points to stick together.

An old and torn paper carrier bag will make a ready to hang picture if one side can be rescued for painting – the inside. Any carriers with handles can replace sacks for races. Hold on and jump! When the handles have gone a self-standing carrier bag makes a good **waste-paper basket**. Stick cut-outs over the name of the shop or over all the bag.

Keep any old picture frames for framing new **works of art**. They can also help put to use plastic bags or sheeting. Pin, tack or peg the plastic tightly to the frame. The plastic can be painted on if you use really thick paint. Powder paint thickened with wall-paper paste or liquid detergent will stick well and can even be washed off!

If the plastic is clear it can be used as a **tracing board**. Support the picture frame slightly from the ground or table and place interesting shapes underneath. Follow the shape on the plastic. Paint lightly!

If powder paint has dried out try putting some drops of hot water on and leave overnight.

How much wood would a woodchuck chuck
If a woodchuck could chuck wood?
He would chuck as much wood as a woodchuck would chuck
If a woodchuck could chuck wood.

Sawn off pieces of wood that have been carefully sanded can have nails or tacks knocked into them and then be used for making **patterns** in clay, plasticine, playdough or pastry. **Knotted string** wound round the wood also makes interesting patterns.

Keep any old bolts, plugs, keys in locks etc., that you can find. Screw them all on to a piece of inch-thick board. Paint the **gadget board** if you want to, but not the gadgets. Other good items are a castor which spins round and also swivels, a hinge, one side only screwed down, or an old bicycle bell.

Old bun trays or egg boxes can be used for a **sorting or matching game**. Paint the hollows different colours, then collect buttons or bits of paper to match the colours. On top of the colours you could add numbers, or shapes such as squares, circles, triangles, to make it more difficult.

Keep buttons off old clothes. They're always an addition to material pictures or **junk montages**. Other uses are: eyes for puppets, wheels, counters, tiddlywinks into egg boxes, sorting into size and colour, replacing lost buttons, putting on to new clothes.

Keep old shirt sleeves for a **tunnel game**. Travel an item down the sleeve giving clues as you go – then out it pops!

Old nylon tights cut into thin strips make the best **stuffing** for knitted or sewn toys, and can be washed.

Old socks make **Christmas stockings or puppets**. A yoghurt carton stuffed down a sock becomes a long nose for a dog, a camel, or a giraffe.

My neck is amazingly, endlessly long,
In colour I'm yellow and brown
I eat the green leaves from the tops of the trees
And still keep my feet on the ground.

What am I?

Yoghurt cartons are good for keeping paint in, or with holes punched in the bottom they make first **pots for seeds**.

Cut two holes side by side in a margarine tub. Stick two fingers through and creep your **snail** along!

Junk items made of tin foil can be kept for: growing things in, holding water or paint, making armour, crowns, cutting up for money.

Save bits of material for **patchwork or applique**. For a patchwork ball you need twelve pentagons. Leave enough opening to stuff it with shredded nylons. With scraps appliqued on to larger pieces of material you could make a baby's first book. Bright simple shapes on each page.

I can think sharply
and I can change:
my colours cover a considerable range.

I can be some mud by
an estuary,
I can be a patch on the bark of a tree.

I can be green grass
or a little thin stone
– or if I really want to be left alone.

I can be a shadow . . .
What I am on your
multi-coloured bedspread, I am not quite sure.

What is it?

A chameleon.

Trying Out

If at first you don't succeed . . .

Have you ever tried not to laugh? Try this:
First person says "ha"
Second person says "ha"
First person says "ha"
Second person says "ha" . . .
Carry on taking turns getting quicker and quicker. Who breaks into real laughter first?

Try saying a nursery rhyme while somebody else says "sausages" after each line:
Jack and Jill went up the hill *sausages*
To fetch a pail of water *sausages*
Jack fell down and broke his crown *sausages*
And Jill came tumbling after *sausages.*

Try saying very quickly:
Susy sells sea shells on the sea shore.

Or, if you can remember it:
Betty bought a bit of butter but she said "My butter's bitter – if I put it in my batter it will make my batter bitter. Better buy some better butter." Betty's mother said she'd let her. So she bought some better butter and she put it in her batter and it made her batter better!

Or, very quickly:
red leather, yellow leather,
red leather, yellow leather.

If you and somebody else both say exactly the same thing at the same time, by accident, you can try making a wish. Link **fingers** and say:
I wish, I wish a very good wish
A very good wish to you,
I wish, a wish a very good wish
I hope your wish comes true.

There's another **wish** with fingers you could try. If you see an eyelash on a friend's cheek gently pick it up on the tip of a licked finger. Turn round so your friend can't see. Hold your hands together, fingers touching, and place the eyelash between the tips of two fingers, any two. Now turn round and your friend holds on to each pair of fingers and makes a wish on each. The pair of fingers that the eyelash was between is the one that might come true. Perhaps somebody will do it for you if you find one of your eyelashes.

Try circling the same finger of each hand in the same direction. Is it easier to circle each of them in an opposite direction?

Hold a finger up in front of you. Look at it. Close your eyes and try to touch the finger with the same finger on the other hand. Now hold up your thumb and try to touch it (eyes closed) with a finger from the other hand.

Can you hold the fingers of one hand up one at a time? Try this, starting with a clenched fist.

Tommy Thumb, Tommy Thumb
Where are you? (pop out thumb)
Here I am
Here I am
How do you do! (bend your thumb)

Peter Pointer, Peter Pointer
Where are you? (pop up index finger)
Here I am
Here I am
How do you do! (bend the finger)

Teddy Tail, Teddy Tail
Where are you? (pop up middle finger)
Here I am
Here I am
How do you do! (bend the finger)

Ruby Ring, Ruby Ring
Where are you? (pop up fourth finger)
Here I am
Here I am
How do you do! (bend the finger)

Baby Small, Baby Small
Where are you? (pop up your little finger)
Here I am
Here I am
How do you do! (bend it then close your fist again)

Fingers all, fingers all
Where are you?
Here we are
Here we are
Ready to wave.

Wave and clap, and now try both hands at the same time.

Fingers have to appear one by one for these rhymes:
Here is the beehive (one hand held tightly round the clenched fist of the other)
But where are the bees?
Hiding away where nobody sees. . . . (slowly move fingers)
Look! They are climbing out of the hive
One, two, three, four, five. (make your fingers appear one by one)

Here is an ant-hill with no ants about
So I called "Please little ants come out"
Then from the ant-hill, answering my call
One, two, three, four, five ants came
And that was all!

In a big town there are not any bees
In the street where I live there are not any trees
But every evening when the sky gets grey
One, two, three, four, five lamps shine
To light the way.

Have you ever been out when the first street lamp lights up? When it gets dark early see if you can notice that happening. Try and catch the first one.

There are a lot of **first things** you can try wishing on: first star seen at night, first strawberry eaten in the year, first bite into wedding, christening or birthday cake, first primrose seen, first mince pie eaten.

There's an old belief that for each mince pie eaten at Christmas you'll have a **lucky** month. Some people say it's the number you eat before the end of the year, others the ones you eat in January.

Sometimes lucky things are baked in cakes. Lucky as long as you don't eat them! In the olden days people had a party on twelfth night (the day to take your decorations down) and baked a big cake with a bean in it. Whoever got the bean was supposed to be lucky. These parties were called beanfeasts! You could try hiding a bean at a beanfeast.

A pinch and a punch for the first of the month
A slap and a kick for being so quick!

Do you remember your dreams when you first wake up?

Friday night's dream
On Saturday told
Is sure to come true
How ever old.

How long can you **balance** on one foot?
If you put one arm behind your back and the other over your shoulder can you touch your fingers?
If you sit on the floor how far can you lean before you fall over?
Is there any part of you you can't reach?

Anthony Ayres
Climbed up the stairs
My shoulder was his bed
But when he wanted room to play
He danced upon my head.

Can you balance a book on your head?
If you can, try walking about with it (no hands!).
Try walking around with a balanced book and coin.
Try balancing a coin on your finger.
Try balancing old paper cups, plates, boxes, and any other junk, on top of one another.

Try this **trick** on someone. On top of a paper cup stick other paper or cardboard things together into a tower. Make it high enough to look as if it might fall any minute. Hold on to the cup and enter a room where your audience are, as if you are keeping the whole thing balanced. Act like a clown in a circus, wobbling and pretending to trip. Then keeping hold of the paper cup let the whole lot fall. Walk out holding the tower upside down!

Here's another trick to try. Stick a small piece of Sellotape over a blown-up balloon. Have a pin ready. Very grandly, say to your audience you are going to perform a very difficult magic trick. Say that you are going to stick a pin in the balloon and it will not burst! Your audience will be full of amazement. Then stick a pin into the middle of the Sellotape. The balloon shouldn't burst. If it does, make sure you stick the Sellotape on well next time.

How **quietly** can you let air out of a balloon?
Try to be absolutely quiet putting buttons into a tin.
Try to be absolutely quiet folding a sheet of newspaper.
See if somebody else can listen really hard to make sure no noise can be heard.
If somebody else does these things and you close your eyes, can you tell which one they are doing?

Try bouncing a ball and catching it in a paper cup. Make a ball and cup **game** out of a stiff paper cone and crumple some newspapers into a ball. Use sticky tape to fix a piece of string inside the cone, tie the other end round the ball. The string should be long enough to let the ball be thrown up and land in the cone. While you're playing this medieval game you could wear a medieval cone hat.
A veil thrown over – it's a hat for a princess. With a few stars and moons stuck on – it's a magician's hat.

Try keeping two hats together. Tie a length of string a few feet long between them. Then you and a friend put them on. Try climbing over and under and through things without losing your hats.

Cut a strip of wall-paper about four inches wide and four feet long. Secure one end under a pile of books. Roll out the other end. Let go. Try to clap and stop the roll before it hits the other end. When you get good at this try touching your nose.

The more you take away from me the bigger I become! What am I?

Tear out a hole in a sheet of newspaper. Turn both round several times and now try to put the torn-out piece of newspaper back so it fits exactly. Try the same with two or three holes. Jumble up the torn-out pieces, before trying to put them back.

Make a hole in a large sheet of newspaper and hang it between two chairs. Try and throw a paper dart through the hole.

If you collect an empty tissue box, a plastic tub cut in half and a ball of plasticine you can make a game. Stick the tub in one half of the box. Put in the ball and try rolling it into the tub. A sweet tube instead of a tub would be more difficult.

Hide some objects under a large piece of material. Can you tell what they are just by looking at them? Can you tell what they are by feeling them? You could put a time limit on this game.

Hide a loud ticking clock in the room and see if it can be found. Give this a time limit too.

Put a pebble, a button or some coins in the bottom of a pail of water. Try hitting them with another pebble, button or a coin.

Attach a long piece of string to a hat that fits securely and on the end of it tie a pencil. Try and get the pencil into a milk bottle without using your hands.

Try to get a cardboard ring over a cardboard roll without knocking the roll over.

Draw different-sized circles on a large piece of paper. Plates, cups and saucers are a good guide for this. Try rolling coins or buttons into them. If you have the top or bottom of a large flat box, tear off one side and put the circled paper into it. It saves retrieving the coins or buttons from the floor.

For another game each player draws some squares on paper, four squares across, four squares down are enough. Two people need to play in turn. One person chooses a square in which to bury his treasure, and makes a small mark on the back of the chosen square. The other person has to guess where the treasure is. "Three squares in from the left, two squares down?" If the answer is "no", make a mark on it. Now it is the other person's turn. Who reaches the treasure first?

Try drawing an outline of something in the air. Can anyone guess what it is?
Can you **draw** a circle without drawing round anything? How good is it?

Try tying some string to the middle of a pencil. Hold the other end of the string down with a finger or a drawing pin (it depends what your surface is) and keeping the string taut take the pencil round in a circle. You should have a good one.

Draw half-way round different sized round things, linking the halves up. You should get a wave or cloud effect. Try making the billows go up and down as well. Now do another line underneath, not necessarily following the top line. Try making other circle patterns.

Try drawing an oval using the same principle as the string-on-pencil circle drawing. Bang two pins or tacks into a board with paper on. Make a loop at one end of a piece of string to go round both tacks, then tie the other end to a pencil. Now, draw carefully, keeping the string taut.

A fairly large piece of board about half an inch thick that you can pin paper on for drawing is useful to have around.

Draw two lines close together. See what else you can make them into just by adding other lines: a railway line, a washing line, a road, a pavement. What else?

Use the lines on corrugated paper to make **prints** with. Cut the paper into shapes and stick on the end of old cotton reels. Try ink or paint patterns. Cut a zig-zag edge on a stiff piece of card and see what patterns you can make in fairly thick paint.

Patterns can be made with paint and paper doilies. Lay the doily on some paper and paint over it. What effect do you have? Leave that paint to dry, lay the doily on in a different place overlapping the first pattern and paint in a different colour. A plastic doily can be used time and time again.

Try cutting your initial out of stiff paper and lay it on a sheet of paper. Now paint or rub over your initial with a wax crayon. Try the same thing with other shapes.

Cut out a piece of tin foil into your initial. Make it small. Put the foil on a slice of bread, toast it, and you will see your initial.

If you are growing marrows you can watch your initial grow. Cut your initial into the marrow when it is still young. Measure it if you like. When the marrow is ready for picking see how big your initial is then!

Make a bubbly mixture with washing-up liquid and add some brightly-coloured powder paint. Froth the mixture up again and lay a piece of paper over the bubbles. Pop, pop, pop and they leave a **pattern**!

If there's any icing left over after decorating a cake, thin it out and smear over a piece of paper. Now drop blobs of paint on the still wet icing sugar. Try mixing different colours of paint.

If you have a large paper plate, stick some pegs round it as if they were the numbers of the clock. Try eight or twelve. Now with some wool **weave** in and out, missing out the same number of pegs in each round. Unwind the wool and try again for a different effect. Change the number of pegs, or change the number to leave out to alter the pattern.

If you have a flower arrangement in a vase, or an ivy plant, try and place it between the sun and a wall so that the **shadow** of the plant is thrown on to the wall. It will need to be fairly near the wall. Now hang or secure a piece of paper on the wall so the shadow falls on to the paper. It doesn't matter if you can't fit the whole shape in. Then draw round the shadow. Colour in later, or just leave as it is. Try other shadow patterns.

Stand in the sun
I am with you.
Stand in the shade
I am gone.
Run out in the sunlight. Go!
Wait. I'm under your big toe!

What am I?

Going Out

Down at the station early in the morning,
See the humming diesels all in a row,
Man in the front seat turns on the engine,
Eee-aaw, brrrr-brrrr, off we go!

For **journeys** by car or train, prepare an animal chart. Down the left-hand side put pictures of the animals you are likely to see. Then draw columns so marks can be put against the animals seen. Before the start of the journey each person could guess which animal they think will be the most abundant.

Make up a story with somebody else, using only one word at a time:
once
upon
a
time
there
was
a
very
large
and so on and so on.

If you take a favourite toy on a journey you could sing this to the tune of "For he's a jolly good fellow".
Bear (or name of toy) *looks out of the window*
Bear looks out of the window
Bear looks out of the window
And what do you think he sees?

He sees a field with sheep in
He sees a field with sheep in
He sees a field with sheep in
That's what bear can see.

Then sing whatever the toy can see next!

• If you are in a car, or have by now managed to empty the carriage of the train, you could say this travelling song.

I travelled over land and sea
And met a man who said to me
An old, old man who said to me,
"*Pray where do you belong to?*"

The answer is related to the type of scenery you are passing.

Oh, I belong to factory land
To factory land, to factory land.
Oh, I belong to factory land
That's where I belong to.

When it's time for the next answer the scenery should have changed.

Trains have a rhythm. With one fist on top of another say:
One potato
Two potato
Three potato
Four
Five potato
Six potato
Seven Potato
More!
One Potato
two potato
Three potato . . .
and so on.

Counting out rhymes have a good rhythm. This one is from California.
Intry, mintry, cutery, corn;
Apple-seed and apple thorn;
Wire, briar, limber, lock;
Three geese in a flock;
One flew east and one flew west;
One flew over the cuckoo's nest.
O.U.T. spells out.

You could clap to this one or tap your feet.

Salt, mustard, vinegar, pepper,
French almond rock,
Bread and butter for your supper
That's all mother's got.
Fish and chips and Coca-Cola
Put them in a pan,
Irish stew and ice cream soda,
We'll eat all we can.

Make up your own rhyming travelling words:

car, far
bus, fuss
train, rain
town, down . . .

For a car journey make a travelling sound bag.
Collect together things which make a noise:
a balloon (flat) that can be pulled, a piece of scrumpled paper, an elastic band round a piece of card, dried peas or beans in a small box, a bunch of keys, two spoons to be hit together – and anything else you can think of. Anybody in the back of the car has to guess what the things are by the sound alone. Then they can make the sounds for the person in the front. You could play this when it is getting too dark to see clearly.

Another game whether it's dark or light is one where you have to close your eyes and say exactly what is happening: turning a corner left or right, slowing down, increasing speed, stopping at a traffic light, a car overtaking you, you overtaking a car or a lorry, coming into a town or leaving one.

If the car induces sleepiness, read the lullaby that Shakespeare's fairies sang to Queen Titania:

You spotted snakes with double tongue
Thorny hedgehogs, be not seen;
Newts and blindworms do not wrong
Come not near our fairy Queen.
Philomel, with melody,
Sing in our sweet lullaby
Lulla, lulla, lullaby; lulla, lulla, lullaby.

Philomel is another name for nightingale.

For a boy there's another passage from the same play:

Be kind and courteous to this gentleman;
Hop in his walks and gambol in his eyes;
Feed him with apricocks and dewberries,
With purple grapes, green figs, and mulberries;
The honey bags steal from the humble-bees,
And, for night-tapers, crop their waxen thighs,
And light them at the fiery glow-worm's eyes,
To have my love to bed and to arise;
And pluck the wings from painted butterflies,
To fan the moonbeams from his sleeping eyes;
Nod to him, elves, and do him courtesies.

There are many kinds of number plate games you can play; looking for a letter at the end of a registration, A, B, C, etc., looking for a number by itself, 2, 4, 7, etc., looking out for letters that make words. Look out for legs – on people or animals, or on pub signs.

Look for magpies by the roadside.
One for sorrow, two for mirth,
Three for a wedding, four for a birth,
Five for silver, six for gold,
Seven for a secret that's never been told.
Often you see only one magpie, but the secret for averting any sorrow is to say "Good-morning Mr Magpie. Good-morning Mr Magpie". Be sure to say it twice and bow while you say it!

Prepare some pieces of newspaper about 300 cm square and fold them in different ways. Tear bits out here and there and see what kind of pattern you have made.
Can you think of a game that involves picking up bits of paper?

What shall we see at a journey's end
The country, the sea, the city, a friend?

Sometimes it's useful to remember some **country** sayings to see if they're right.

When the wind is in the East
Tis neither good for man nor beast.

When the wind is in the North
The skilful fisher goes not forth.

When the wind is in the South
It blows the bait in the fish's mouth.

When the wind is in the West,
Then it is at its very best.

When the dew is on the grass
Rain will never come to pass.

Rain before seven
Fair by eleven.

St Swithin's day, if thou dost rain,
For forty days it will remain
St Swithin's day, if thou be fair,
For forty days 'twill rain na mair.
St Swithin's day is 15 July.

If the moon is on its back
It holds the water in its lap
If the moon stands on its end
Then the rain will all descend.

Candlemass day, 2 February,
is also a significant weather day.
If candlemass day be fair and bright
Winter will have another flight
But if candlemass day brings cloud and rain
Winter will not come again.

Weather permitting, look out for catkins.
A catkin tied to a piece of string
Makes a creepy crawly thing!

It started right up here
And crept behind my ear
Then round my neck
And on to my shoulder
It had a think, and then got bolder
And slid down to my elbow but
It never paused but on it went
Across my hand to my fingertips
A very tickly, tickly, itch.

Go out
When the wind's about;
Let him buffet you
Inside out.

Go out
In a rainy drizzle;
Never sit by the fire
To sizzle.

Go out
When the snowflakes play;
Toss them about
On the white highway.

Go out
And stay till night;
When the sun is shedding
Its golden light.

Look out for a farmer sowing seeds.
One to rot,
One to grow,
One for the pigeon,
One for the crow.

Have you ever noticed rooks' nests high up in the branches of trees? Twigs in the middle of twigs!

Collect **twigs** that have small fircones on. These can be used for kindling or for dried flower arrangements. Keep some for Christmas and spray them with gold or silver paint for table decorations.

Twigs make a good support for flowers in vases. Break up the twigs into small pieces and put them in a jumbled fashion into a vase.

Fairly straight twigs can be kept for a game of pick-a-sticks. You toss a small pile into the air and leave them where they've landed. Then, with a stick to help you, see how many twigs you can flick or pick off without disturbing any of the others.

If the twigs have small forks on them, try building a twig tower using the forks to balance and lock with one another.

Tie very tiny twigs together to make a broom for a toy. Pine needles would be as good. Make a witch's broom for yourself.

Make two twigs into a cross and bind them with wool. Weave other coloured lengths of wool round this frame by passing over and under the twigs. When finished you could hang this on another length of wool so it could be a necklace.

Make a weaving pattern to hang on a wall. Stick three or four twigs into a strip of plasticine. Weave wool in and out, backwards and forwards. When you've finished remove the sticks from the plasticine, turn on its side and hang.

Whether the weather be fine,
Or whether the weather be not,
Whether the weather be cold,
Or whether the weather be hot,
We'll weather the weather,
Whatever the weather,
Whether we like it or not!

Collect twigs of forsythia, flowering currant, hazel, and, when ready, lilac and sticky (horse chestnut) buds. Keep them in water in a warm dark place and they will come out long before those outside. You can watch sticky buds unfold day by day.

Lo, the winter is past,
The rain is over and gone,
The flowers appear on the earth,
The time of the singing birds is come. . . .

Listen for the first cuckoo.
In April I open my bill
In May I come to stay
In June I change my tune
In July away I fly
In August go I must.

When daisies pied and violets blue
And ladysmocks all silver-white
And cuckoo buds of yellow hue
Do paint the meadow with delight ...
The cuckoo then on every tree, sings "cuckoo, cuckoo".
"Pied" means two colours, hence "magpies" and the "pied" piper!

See if you can notice **birds** building their nests. Or see them carrying small twigs, feathers or bits of material.
Wood pigeons may sound as if they're saying:
Two sticks across and a little bit of moss
It will doooo. It will doooo. It will doooo.
A chaffinch sounds as if it's saying: *pink, pink, pink*, or: *no little birds can pick up seeds as I can.*
A yellow hammer says: *a little bit of bread and no cheese.*
And the pessimistic blackbird: *rain all day, rain all day.*

63

Can you name any birds? Try to recognise a robin, starling, blackbird and thrush. In July and August watch out for scruffy-looking birds. Robins lose their tails altogether for about a week and look very odd wobbling on thin legs. When the adult birds don't have to work so hard gathering food, and all the fledgelings have left the nest, they grow new feathers and look quite tidy again.

A tip for bird feeding. It's not good to put bread out after March, as baby birds cannot digest it easily. If there is a long drought birds find the worms impossible to catch (they've gone down too deep in order to find water), so bits of fat and table scraps can help them out.

The north wind doth blow,
And we shall have snow,
And what will poor robin do then?
Poor thing.
He'll sit in a barn,
And keep himself warm,
And hide his head under his wing,
Poor thing.

See what else you can find. **Wild flowers** that you can pick are cow parsley, also known as Queen Anne's lace, and white dead-nettle. The nettles don't sting and have a pretty white flower at the top. Strip away all the leaves, put in a vase, and people think you have exotic lilies. Poppies and bluebells will live if the stems are singed as soon as they are gathered. Press flowers between blotting paper and under a pile of heavy books.

Can you spot a red admiral or a cabbage white? They're **butterflies**. Walk very quietly and watch out for other small creatures. You may find discarded snail shells. Can you make up another name for a snail? In Suffolk it's called a hod-me-dod.

Brown and furry
Caterpillar in a hurry;
Take your walk
To the shady leaf or stalk

May no toad spy you,
May the little birds pass by you,
Spin and die,
To live again a butterfly.

Can you find a **footprint**? What animal do you think it belongs to? A cow, a horse? If there is mud around you may be able to detect bird prints or even a rabbit print! Watch out for rabbit holes!

See how many different **grasses** you can collect. They look nice in a vase when you get them home. Teazels can become hedgehogs. Stick currants on the spikes for a nose and eyes. Snip the spikes flat on one side and he'll sit still.

Can you tell the difference between oats, wheat and barley? Pick a few ears of each to mix with your grasses.

Oats and beans and barley grows,
Oats and beans and barley grows,
But you nor I nor nobody knows
How oats and beans and barley grows.

First the farmer sows his seed
Then he stands and takes his ease,
Stamps his feet and claps his hands
And turns around to view his lands.

You have to yell "oh" at the end to scare the birds away!

Around July look on an oak tree for gall-wasps. Their other name is oak apples. They look like very small green apples. Take one off the tree and open it up. What do you find inside?

On roses you could also find "robins' pin cushions". They look like tiny green and scarlet hedgehogs. Like the gall-wasps they're made by a tiny insect.

What do you suppose?
A bee sat on my nose
Then what do you think?
He gave me a wink
And said "I beg your pardon!
I thought you were my garden."

If you have a hydrangea bush in the **garden** you can pick the flower heads to dry. Hang them upside down so the air can circulate around them. They can then be mixed with dried grasses, teazels, honesty, and ears of corn.

Pick lavender early in the morning and hang to dry. Then strip the flower heads from the stems and keep in a paper bag until you want to use them.
Here's a mixture for making into lavender bags:
Two tablespoons of lavender
One tablespoon of dried tyme
One tablespoon of grated dried lemon rind.
For the bags cut out shapes of material and sew with a running stitch round the edge. Turn inside out leaving a hole to put the lavender in. Finish by oversewing the hole and decorate with a ribbon bow, or perhaps a loop to hang it up by.

Roses are red, diddle diddle, lavender's blue
If you will have me, diddle diddle, I will have you.
Lilies are white, diddle diddle, rosemary's green
When you are king, diddle diddle, I will be queen.

From garden, park or country collect autumn **leaves** of different colour and shape.
Firm flat leaves can be used for shoe-polish prints any time of the year. Choose leaves with marked veining and smooth brown shoe polish over the underside of the leaf. Prepare the paper you are going to make the print on by covering it with wax crayon (it's best to lay the paper over a rough surface such as wood or a wall and use the whole length of the crayon). Now place the leaf gently down on this and smooth all over. Peel off the leaf very carefully. Lay down another leaf and build up a picture.

Any leaves that are brightly coloured can be placed against a window so that the light shines through them. Put them in wax bags or wax paper and seal by gently pressing with a cool iron. Do this to several leaves and build up a patchwork quilt to hang against a window.

Flowers first, then petals fall,
Until there's not one left at all.

Then day by day, the berries grow,
Until the hedgerows burn and glow.

There are hips and haws – like bright red beads,
And inside, warm and safe lie – seeds.

In autumn look for **seeds** of all kinds. From the trees find sycamore seeds, chestnuts and acorns. From the flowers find poppy heads full of seeds. Seeds that look like wisps of grey cotton wool are on wild clematis, called "Old Man's Beard".
How do you think some seeds get scattered?
There are seeds in fruits too. If you are collecting blackberries be careful of eating them after St Michael's Day, 29 September. There's a saying which says that after that day the devil has put his hoof in them.

Collect acorn cups to make flowers for a miniature garden. Stick the stalks in plasticine and, if you want to, screw up brightly-coloured bits of tissue paper and stick inside the cup. If you find a cup with a really long stem you could use it as a toy's soup ladle or pipe.

If you want to grow flowers from seeds, let the flower head die naturally then dry the seeds well. Keep them in labelled envelopes until you want to use them, and when spring comes round sow them in yoghurt pots and put them in a warm place.

Five small seeds planted in a row
Down comes the rain, the seeds begin to grow.
Out comes the sun the buds begin to show
Five small flowers planted in a row.

On a beach what can you find
Besides the sea and sand?
Things that the sea leaves behind
And gives back to the land.

Beachcomb for: cork, bits of old rubber tyres, wood, old shoes, glass balls, pieces of old net, polystyrene, glass bottles, plastic bottles. Any messages?

On a beach what can you find
Besides the sea and sand?
Things that people leave behind
Bottles, bags and cans.

Perhaps you could help clear up things like that.

On a beach what can you find
Besides the sea and sand?
Things that the tide leaves behind
From the rocks, and underwater land.

Collect things for a beach montage: shells, crabs, starfish, sea urchins, pebbles, seaweed.
What happens if you hold seaweed under water?

My fingers are grass
Now watch the wind blow
Blow, blow, blow,
Or perhaps they are seaweed under the sea
And here is a fish looking round for its tea.

Make an outline with pebbles.

How would you like to be me
Deedle, deedle, dee
Tossing about in the sea
Deedle, deedle, dee
Covered in seaweedle, deedle, dee
How would you like to be me
Deedle, deedle, dee.

Prepare a **shop chart**. Draw or stick on pictures of bread, cakes, vegetables, fruit, meat, etc. on the left, with columns where you can tick what is needed on the right. As you go shopping refer to the chart to see that everything has been bought.

Added interest for shopping could be **spotting cards**. Down one side of a piece of paper draw the most common road signs: 30 mph speed limit, Parking, Traffic Lights, No Entry, Stop, Crossroads . . .
How many can you spot?

Another card could have pictures of building features peculiar to your town or village: a round, arched or square window, a church spire, a weathervane, a clock, a statue, a signpost . . .
Can you manage to see them all on one shopping expedition?

What about **first one to see** . . . a policeman, postman, postbox, dog, baby in a buggy, cat, a shopping basket on wheels, a red umbrella!

Slim, silver splinters of grey rain
Have stabbed November gloom
And all along the streets again
Umbrellas are in bloom.

On stiff, upstanding stems they sway
And bob and billow by,
And most of them are primly grey
Or black as ebony.

But some are blue and some are brown
And some are rowan red
A thousand flowers to light the town
When other flowers are dead.

A thousand opening buds to greet
The grey November rain
Then sing – oh sing in every street –
Umbrellas bloom again.

Can you tell by the clouds if it's going to rain?
Can you tell by the clouds which way the wind is blowing?
Look for your shadow. Is it there when the sun is behind a cloud? Is it longer at the end of the day than at the time you have your midday meal?

Keep a **weather calendar**.
On a strip of paper draw square pictures of the weather: rain, snow, wind, sun, clouds. Make a square hole as big as the pictures in another piece of paper. Two slits above and below the square means you can slide the "window" up and down the strip of paper to show whichever weather is appropriate. If you make a hole in the top of the strip you can hang it up!

If you go for a **walk** in the town or the country what can you hear?
Can you hear: the wind in the trees, cars or aeroplanes, a phone ringing, a baby crying, a dog barking, birds singing?
What happens if a road compressor starts to work?
When it's quiet again can you hear a twig crack underfoot or a leaf rustle. Perhaps a police car or fire-engine comes along!
Make up your own story using the sounds to tell it.

The chestnut trees are a market square
The bees are busy merchants there.
The chestnut flowers are blazing flares
And the leaves umbrellas to shade the wares.
The oaks are a parliament grand and grave
The beeches make a cathedral nave.
The larches and limes are a garden grove
Where the ladies who live in the birches rove.
The poplars, whispering dark deceit
Are numerous houses in scandal street.
The ashes and elms in long straight roads
Are serious statesmen's proud abodes.
The city walls are double lines
Of rank protecting firs and pines
And, slipping unseen through leafy seas
Wind is King in the town of trees.

Finding Out

How many pips in an apple,
How many apples on a tree,
How many trees in an orchard,
How many orchards standing free?

So many waves in the ocean,
So many pebbles on the shore,
How many swirls as the waves toss and curl,
As they whisper, as they roar?

There are many things you'll never find the answer to but you may be able to find out some answers to the following. Why? How does it happen? How does it work?

Find some boxes that are put together without being stuck; a tea bag box, a box with a twirly end that holds disposable washing-up cloths, a cake box, an egg box with a flap that loops round and under itself to do up. Undo the boxes as much as you can and see if you can do them up again.

A lot of egg boxes with flaps could be fixed together to make a monster.

Find boxes of different sizes and see whether they will all fit one inside another. If you take them out again will they fit inside one another a different way, or does it have to be the same again?

Can you fold a piece of paper in half more than seven times? Does the size or the thickness of the paper make any difference?

If you hold a piece of card at one corner it stays flat and straight.

Hold the same-sized piece of newspaper in one corner. What happens? How small does the newspaper have to be before it will stay straight?

If you have a big piece of card, wobble it about and see what sort of **sound** it makes. Do different sorts of card or paper make different noises?

Tap on an empty box. Now fill it up with material and tap again. Is the noise different?

Put an elastic band on a piece of card so that the card is flat. Twang it. What sort of noise does it make? Then bend the card, and twang again. Does it make a different noise?

What sort of sound does an elastic band round a box make? Put a thick elastic band and a thin elastic band round a box. Do they make different sounds?

Do different bits of wood make different sounds? With your knuckle go round carefully tapping pieces of wooden furniture, even the door! Do you notice any change in the sound?

If you can collect sawn-off branches from a tree or left-over wood from a building, see if you can make different sounds almost like notes on a piano. Test this by hitting them with something hard like a wooden spoon. Put the lowest-sounding one near your left hand and the next lowest next, and so on, until you have the highest-sounding wood at the top on your right. You've made your own xylophone!

Jeremiah have a care
How you sit upon your chair
Count the legs, 1, 2, 3, 4
See that all are on the floor.

Collect pebbles and stones and see if they make different sounds. Maybe you need to hit them with something mad of metal?

How did the music of the world begin?
Did it start with a whistle or a violin?
With a parp, parp, parp,
Or the twankle of a harp.
Or the booming of the big bass drum?
Or did the wind through the branches swaying
Whisper the words of a song?
Did the rustling reeds
And the buzzing bees
Sing a tune we have loved so long?
That's how the music of the world began.
Then a fiddle
And a whistle
And an old tin pan
A parp, parp, parp,
And the twankle of a harp
And the boom of the big bass drum.
That's how the music of the world began
Then a fiddle
And a whistle
And an old tin pan
A parp, parp, parp
And the booming of the big bass drum.

Water Will a pebble float? Will a piece of sawn-off wood float? Will a twig float? Will a piece of wood with a hole in it float?

Find as many things as you can that have holes in them: curtain rings, cotton reels, pastry cutters, keys with a hole in the end, perhaps a kitchen utensil such as a sieve that hangs by a wire loop. See if you can blow bubbles through the holes. Can you blow a bubble through an oval shape? Does the shape of the hole make any difference to the bubble?

How much water will a sponge hold? A jam jar full? A bucket full?

Water has no taste at all
Water has no smell,
Water's in the waterfall
In pump and tap and well.
Water's everywhere about:
Water's in the rain,
In the bath, the pond, and out
At sea it's there again.

How could you pour water from a wide-necked container, such as a pudding basin, into a milk bottle without spilling it? Would a stiff paper cone help?

Pour water into a jam jar until it is about three-quarters full. Without adding any more water, make the water reach the top of the jam jar! You can have a sponge, some pebbles, some newspaper and some flour. Which do you think will help you solve your problem?

Put some more water in a jam jar and carefully draw round the line of the water with a wax crayon. Now tip the jam jar up on one side. Put one edge on a book. What happens to the water? Tip up the other side of the jam jar. What happens now? If you went on following the line of the water with crayon you might get quite a nice pattern.

If you have an old glass jar, such as an empty coffee jar, a cork, a **magnet**, and a few tacks or nails, you could make a diving bell. Stick as many nails into the cork as are needed to make the cork just float. If the cork has a thicker end, put the nails in that. How do you make the bell dive? Well, there's this magnet . . .

What will a magnet's force pull through? Glass? Paper? Material? Air? Water?

Hold a mirror in front of a torch. Can you see a blob of light anywhere else in the room?

Twinkle, twinkle little star
How I wonder what you are!
Up above the world so high
Like a diamond in the sky.

If you hold a pencil half in and half out of water does it look different?

If you see a puddle look down into it. Does anything happen to your shape? Does it look like you? Are you upside down or the right way up? If you step in it, wearing your wellingtons, can you make prints on the ground?

If you mix water with any of the following things: sand, soil, powder paint, modelling plaster or cellulose filler, what happens to them?

Make a **print** of a crescent moon. Paint a thick gooey moon that leans on one side. Press a clean bit of paper over it. When you lift it off you have a print of the moon. Is it exactly the same? Try some other shapes. Does the same thing happen if you lay another sheet of paper over it?

Lovely moon, lovely moon
What do you see
As you look down upon
Meadow and tree?
I see a lamb
I see a sheep
I see a child
Going to sleep.

Drop blobs of wet paint on to wet paper. What happens? Sprinkle dry powder paint on to wet paper. Does it make a different effect?

Make a printing block for yourself. Mix some plaster into a smooth, fairly thick consistency and put it into a flat polystyrene food tray. When it is set, carefully take it out and paint over the smoothest side. Then with a pencil draw a simple outline of something you like. With a small screwdriver scratch out the plaster where the pencil lines are so you leave a small indentation. Now smear paint or ink all over the block and press on to clean paper. Does what you have drawn in pencil appear on the paper? Is it facing the same way round?

Fold a piece of paper in half and open it out. Drop blobs of paint on just one half of the paper. Then fold it again and press with your hand. Open the paper. What result do you get? Are both sides the same?

Fly fly fly butterfly
Fly and flutter, flutter and fly
Fly, fly, fly butterfly
Fly and flutter
Flutter and fly.
On any kind of day
Your pretty wings look gay
As you fly fly
Fly butterfly
Fly
Fly and flutter
Flutter and fly.

Hold a small mirror half-way across a picture of a butterfly. Do you still see the whole butterfly? Move the mirror to the edge of the butterfly. How many butterflies can you see now? Tape two mirrors together and hold at right angles round the butterfly. Can you see even more butterflies?

Do all these things now with more pictures. What happens if you hold the mirror half-way across the picture of a cat? Or a worm? Or a football? Or a clock?

Paint, when it is dry, sticks to paper and won't scrape off. Does wax stick on wax?

On a piece of tough paper draw swirling blocks of bright colour with wax crayons. Now completely cover this with black wax crayon. With the end of a broken pencil or a knitting needle scratch away the black wax into patterns or the outline of something. What do you find happens when you scratch the black wax away?

Hold an orange up to your eye and look out of the window. Does the orange look as if it's bigger than a car outside? Bigger than another house?

Hold your thumb up. Does that look bigger than things outside?

Try looking at the place where you live when you can still see it but are some distance away. Hold up your thumb – is it bigger? Or does it just look as if it is?

If somebody is walking towards you, do they look as if they get bigger? What happens if they walk away?

Air is all around you, air is everywhere!

Hold a strip of thin paper in front of your mouth and say: *Peter Piper picked a peck of pickled pepper*. What happens to the paper?
Say: *Pretty Polly*. What happens?
Now say: *Sally saw her sister sewing*. What happens to the paper?
See if you can say different things, some which make the paper move, some which don't. Why do you think the paper moves for some words but not for others?

Can you make the air around you move faster? Hold a square piece of paper in front of your face. Don't move yourself or the paper. Can you feel anything? Now wave the paper up and down. Can you feel anything now? Does the paper move the air around more quickly if you fold the paper backwards and forwards into a fan?

Do a test to see whether there is dust in the air around you. In a baking tray put a piece of clean paper and hold it down with a stone. Now leave this outside, under shelter in case it rains, and in a day or two go and see how clean the paper is.

Will air hold up a tiny bit of tissue? Can you help by blowing?
Tie four cotton threads to the corners of a paper tissue and tie the other ends to a small ball of newspaper. Let it drop from a reasonable height. Does this help the piece of tissue to stay up longer? Would the parachute work better if there was something a bit heavier on the end of it?

When all the washing-up liquid has gone out of its bottle, close the tiny lid down and squeeze the bottle close to your face. Can you hear anything or feel anything? Now open the lid and press the bottle. What do you feel and hear? Can you blow your hair about?
Can you keep a piece of tissue up in the air?

What's inside an empty tin?
What do you blow when you blow?
What do you breathe both out and in
How does a kite fly high or low?
Air, air, air is everywhere,
Out in the street or in a room
Air, air, air is everywhere
In the tyres of a car or a bright balloon.

Remove the top of a washing-up liquid bottle and in its place snap on an unblown-up balloon. Squeeze the bottle gently. What happens to the balloon? Now squeeze the bottle hard. What happens this time?

Have you ever had enough puff to blow over a very heavy book? Stand the book up and try. No touching! Just a big blow! No luck? Try again, and place a paper bag under the edge of the book. Blow into the paper bag and see what happens! Why do you think the bag helps?

Fill a large bowl with water. Into a plastic beaker or mug put a dry piece of material or paper. Make sure it will stay in the bottom of the mug. Now plunge the mug upside down into the bowl of water. Will the contents of the mug be wet? You find out!

Fill up a mug with water so the water reaches right to the top. Now slide a thin piece of card carefully over the top of the mug. Hold the card with the flat of your hand and turn the mug and card upside down. Take your hand away! Does the card fall off and the water fall out? This is best found out over the sink otherwise you could find yourself finding out how much water a mop will hold!

A far more gentle surprise is a **cress pot** surprise. Soak a small pottery flower pot (not plastic) until it is very wet. Soak the cress seeds in a saucer of water. Put the wet seeds all over the inside of the wet pot and stand the pot upside down in a saucer of water. Take a look each day. Within a week the cress will start to find the light.

I had a little nut tree,
Nothing would it bear
But a silver nutmeg
And a golden pear;

The King of Spain's daughter
Came to visit me,
And all for the sake
Of my little nut tree.

I skipp'd over water,
I danced over sea,
And all the birds in the air
Couldn't catch me.

If you want to watch how a **bean** grows whether it is upside down or not, find a clear glass jar. Make a roll of newspaper or blotting paper and put it inside the jar. Fill the middle with soil or cotton wool. Keep this moist all the time the beans are growing. Slip beans – either broad or runner bean seeds – around the jar between the glass and the paper placing some with the dark bit to the top, and some with the dark bit facing down. Watch what happens.

It's worth finding out if you can grow your own tree. Chestnuts and avacados, lemon and orange pips are best potted and forgotten, but an acorn is something that you can watch. Save a dark tablet jar (the kind that holds yeast), fill it with water to the top and place the acorn on the rim so it is just touching the water. Seal round the top of the jar with a bit of foil. Wait until the roots are well established, then transfer to soil.

Run a comb against your hair. Now try picking up a bit of tissue. Will your comb pick up anything else? Try small pieces of cotton, paper or silver paper. Does a lollipop stick or a pencil have the same effect?

When you are in the dark and you take something off that you are wearing do you sometimes see sparks and hear a "snip-snap" noise? Have you noticed which of your clothes it happens to? Find out what they're made of.

The same thing can sometimes happen when you brush your hair or stroke a cat. Imagine it happening a thousand times bigger. It does happen. What do you think it could be?

Without any legs I run for ever –
This is the spell of the mighty river.

I fall for ever and not at all –
This is the spell of the waterfall.

Without a voice I roar aloud –
This is the spell of the thunder-cloud.

99

Have you found out yet the things you like doing best?

Do you like to jump in puddles
Do you like to blow big bubbles
Sail ducks or boats in your bath
See funny things which make you laugh
Play games of hide and seek
Say out loud the days of the week
Do you like to clap your hands together
Paint a picture of the weather
What about a ride in a train
A loving kiss when you've got a pain
Do you like to have a ball to throw
Say hello to someone you know.

Building towers
Saying boo
Stroking a cat
Presents for you
Zebedee
Little Ted
Flying a kite
Being snug in bed
Wobbly jellies
Riding a bike
Are any of these things
The things you like?

If not, find out what *you* like!

Helping Out

Out you go, out you go,
Heavy as lead,
Up you hang, up you hang,
Overhead.
Now start dancing
Till you are dried
Then back in the basket and inside.

Sorting out afterwards can be a great help: socks in pairs, things that need ironing, things that don't, folding those that don't, damping down and rolling those that do.

For a game deliberately mix up pairs of gloves, socks and shoes. Hide one sock, glove or shoe, or one of each. The missing items have to be found when all the pairs have been paired up.

How many pairs of things can you think of?

If things need washing they could be sorted out into appropriate washing piles: whites, coloureds, hand wash.

Rub-a-dub-dub
Three men in a tub
And who do you think they be?
The butcher, the baker,
The candle-stick maker.
Turn them out
Knaves all three!

Hide several small items in a bowl of **soapy water**. Things that are familiar and some things that are not. Can you feel what they are under the soap?

Hands are very handy things,
Hands can wash things,
Hands can squash things,
Hands can gently pat your head.
Hands can clap,
Hands can flap,
Hands can point like this or that
Hands can make things,
Hands can shake things,
Hands can flutter, just like wings.
Hands can fold,
Hands can hold,
Hands are very handy things.

When you're helping by washing baby's toys or your own, try blowing bubbles through your hands. Make a hole with your thumbs and first fingers. Then try a smaller hole, just the space between the thumb and first finger of one hand.

A bubble grows bigger and bigger
Blow very gently
Treat it with care!
Larger and larger
Then all of a sudden –
With hardly a sound
It's no longer there.

Odd bits of soap can be saved and stuck together with water.
If you cut up thin bits of foam rubber into heart or interesting shapes and sew the edges over with cotton you could put the bits of soap inside. Use this for washing yourself or your toys.

Scouring out the porridge pot
Round and round and round!

Out with all the scraith and scoopery,
Lift the eely ooly droopery,
Chase the glubbery slubbery gloopery
Round and round and round!

Out with all the doleful dithery,
Ladle out the slimy slithery,
Hunt and catch the hithery thithery,
Round and round and round!

Out with all the obbly gubbly,
On the stove it burns so bubbly,
Use the spoon and use it doubly,
Round and round and round!

From washing up to **tidying up**!

Toys on wheels can be made to go into a box. Get a long box from the supermarket or a flower shop. Cut holes in one side big enough for cars to go through. Send the cars to the garages when they're in need of servicing!

A captain of a ship can get most things done when he wants them done. Sing this to the music of "The big ship sails on the Illy Ally O".

The captain says dust the table and the chairs,
Dust the table and the chairs
Dust the table and the chairs,
The Captain says dust the table and the chairs
He, hi, illy ally O!

The captain says make your bed and smooth the sheets,
Fold and smooth your sheets
Fold and smooth your sheets,
The captain says make your bed and smooth the sheets
He, hi, illy ally O!

The captain says wash and dry the dishes well,
Wash and dry them well
Wash and dry them well,
The captain says wash and dry the dishes well
He, hi, illy ally O!

From now on make up your own verses for whatever needs doing!

Wash the dishes, wipe the dishes,
Ring the bell for tea;
Three good wishes, three good kisses,
I will give to thee.

Before dusting or after dusting is a good time to remind you of Mr Duster, who has often appeared on Play School. Nancy Quayle has been involved in the programme since its inception, and the theory behind her idea and presentation of Mr Duster is the basis on which **puppets** are used in the programme. We present one of her stories here:

Each story must be introduced by the plain duster, and end with the plain duster.
The underlying purpose is to help children begin to realise the difference between truth and fantasy, and that by the power of their imagination life is given to an inanimate object.

This is an ordinary duster made of blue and white check cotton with a useful loop of tape to hang it up (show duster and loop).

We are going to make him into a little man. What does he want first? A head (ties large knot). *And what does he have on his head? A hat* (leave corner sticking up).

My first finger is Mr Duster's neck (thrust it into knot), *my thumb is one arm* (thumb draped in duster), *and my second finger is his other arm* (drape second finger in duster). Always waggle bare fingers and thumb before making them into arms and neck, so that when Mr Duster moves and talks, no child, however young, can think it is alive. Mr Duster has a growling voice.

Mr Duster has got a friend, Mrs Scarf. (A scarf quite unlike Mr Duster. It is rather difficult to make her, with Mr Duster helping, but it can be managed.)
One day Mr Duster heard a knock at the door, and there was Mrs Scarf.
Mr Duster "*Good morning Mrs Scarf.*"
Mrs Scarf "*Oh, Mr Duster – can you lend me an umbrella? I want to go for a walk in my new hat and it has begun to rain.*"

Mr Duster produces umbrella. (An umbrella can be made out of a circle of paper stuck on top of a lollipop stick). They discuss where they will go – to look at shops, to feed the ducks in the park, depending on your own recent experiences.
"*Well, Mr Duster, the time has come.*"
(Mr Duster) "*What time?*"
"*The time for you to be a duster again.*" (Mr Duster droops and puts his head in his hands.) "*There's no need for you to be sad. You know we can make you into a little man again whenever we like.*" (Mr Duster looks up and claps his hands.)
"*Wave goodbye*" (Mr Duster waves). *Now, off with his head* (unties knot), *take away his arms, and he is a duster again, with a useful loop of tape to hang him up.*

Other Mr Duster stories will no doubt occur to you from particular situations.

Time for cooking

You could help turn plain biscuits into something for a special treat by putting on bits of glacé cherry as a mouth and eyes. Arrange a chocolate or icing sugar hairline then stick the faces into individual trifles or blancmanges.

Help mix a jelly for orange wedges.
Cut as many oranges as you need in half. Squeeze out their juice and strain it (just for the pips). Using a tangerine or orange jelly and the juice, make a very stiff jelly and pour it into the orange halves. Leave the halves to set, and then cut them into wedges which can be eaten with your fingers.

I eat my peas with honey
I've done it all my life:
It makes the peas taste funny,
But it keeps them on the knife.

You could make animal shapes with pastry. Pull and push the dough into round fat animals or cut out flat shapes. What about an elephant, a fish, a bird or a duck?

Behold the duck
It does not cluck,
A cluck it lacks.
It quacks.
It is specially fond
Of a puddle or a pond.
When it dines or sups,
It bottom ups.

Would your duck like an Easter birds' nest?
Crumble up some shredded wheat until it is in separate shreds. Put one tablespoon of water in a pan and then put in a small bar of chocolate. Melt over a low heat. Then stir in the wheat until all the shreds are covered in chocolate. Mould them into a nest and put on a plate or wire tray to harden. Fill them up with marzipan or sugar eggs.

If you are tired of all this real cooking you could invent a little something of your own.

A pound of stones and a bicycle clip,
A toy soldier and a potato chip,
A spoonful of sugar, a spoonful of sand,
For the sweetest supper in all the land!

Four woolly socks and one, two, three
Fresh green leaves from the boojoo tree.
Two tin taps, one pot of paste,
For the finest feast you'll ever taste!

A peanut, a paint pot, plastic fruit,
A small green book and a welly boot,
Salt and pepper, a cotton reel,
For a truly mouthwatering scrumptious meal!

113

Quietly please

Sometimes it's a help if you can be quiet or play or do things by yourself. First you might need to let off a bit of steam.

Creeping quietly through the jungle,
Stretching out an enormous paw,
Sitting still and quietly watching
Quickly pouncing with a roar!

Bang on an upturned tin with a wooden spoon. Crash two baking trays together. Turn a hand whisk in an empty bowl.

There was a man called Michael Finnagen
He kicked up an awful dinnagen
Because they said he must not singagen
Poor old Michael Finnagen, beginagen!

Be quiet with somebody else. You can "sing", mouthing the words of a well-known rhyme or song. Can the other person guess what it is?

A quiet game which needs preparation is newspaper secrets. With a white candle draw pictures on newspaper. The secrets will be discovered when brushed over with thin water paint.

Make **mobiles** for yourself or a friend. If your drinking straws aren't all chewed up when you've finished drinking, dry them out. Then thread three together at a time and tie them into a triangle. Make another one and place it over the top of the first triangle so you have a star shape. If you stick them together and make some more you could hang them from a wire coat hanger as a mobile.

Tear off the bumps from cardboard egg boxes. Paint them bright colours. Then string several bumps together. To keep them slightly apart from each other tie a knot in the thread then put on another bump, then tie another knot and so on. Hang all the lengths of bumps on to a wire coat hanger and hang near an open window. The bottom bumps could have thin strips of tissue or silver tinsel stuck to them.

Draw a lot of different-sized **spirals**. With some, cut round the line to the middle. Attach the middle end to cotton and hang up. It should bounce up and down in the breeze. Other spirals can be turned into snails by drawing a head and horns.

Cut out very simple animal shapes and hang them on cotton. Thread the cotton, some short, some long, and tie to a wire coat hanger. Simple outlines are best: fish, chickens and elephants.

The elephant is a graceful bird,
It flits from twig to twig,
It builds its nest in a rhubarb tree,
And whistles like a pig.

Stick bits of cotton wool on to a sheet of paper and turn them into sheep by adding legs and heads. Or turn them into flowers, blossom on a tree, or fluffy chickens. Even strange men from Jupiter may have woolly bodies.

Roll pages of old magazines round a knitting needle or pencil and stick the edge with wallpaper paste. Cut up the roll into different lengths. You've now got **beads** to thread and make into necklaces or bracelets.

A cotton reel rattle would be much appreciated by a **baby**. Wash the cotton reels and take all the paper off, then thread them on to washable ribbon. Tie the ribbon together at the end.

Help amuse a baby or someone young by playing on their fingers and toes with these rhymes.

This can brew and this can bake,
This can make a wedding cake,
This can make a wedding ring,
And this one can do anything! (little finger or toe)

Once a man
Walked on my toes,
Along my legs,
Up to my nose,
Go away! I said,
And so he jumped on to my head.

Apple pie, apple pie,
. . . . likes apple pie,
So do I, so do I, so do I.

Start by tickling round and round a palm then run your fingers up the arm to the armpit.

With a child on your lap, sway your knees from side to side. Use the child's name.

Joseph, Joseph, how do you ride?
Slowly like this, from side to side?
Joseph, Joseph, how do you go?
up so (bounce knees)
up so
high (if strong enough pick child up)
and low (open legs and lower child between them).

Go to sleep, little sheep
On the hay, soft and deep,
While the quiet stars peep,
Go to sleep, little sheep.

You could help make **Christmas decorations** such as a Christmas is coming ring. Cover a sandwich baking tin with silver foil. Press four lumps of plasticine round the tin and stick in each a candle. Surround the candles with evergreen leaves, holly berries and cones. The idea is to light one candle at teatime on the fourth Sunday before Christmas, two candles on the third Sunday, three on the second and four on the last.
Don't forget to blow them out when tea is finished. You can light them all again on Christmas day.

Bounce buckram velvets dear,
Christmas comes but once a year,
Bounce buckram velvets dear,
Christmas comes but once a year.

Christmas comes but once a year,
But when it does it brings good cheer,
Christmas comes but once a year,
But when it does it brings good cheer.

Always fireproof cones and evergreens if you are using them with candles. You need:
One pound of boric acid
One and half pound of borax
Two gallons of water
Mix the boric acid and borax together, dry, then add the water. Stir thoroughly every time you use it. Evergreens can be dropped in and Christmas trees sprayed with this mixture.

Another decoration using your own bits and pieces can be made in a scallop shell. Stand a candle on a lump of plasticine stuck into the shell. Put berries and cones round it. You could add small glass balls (the ones that have lost their wire) or even ribbon. If the shell is unsteady prop it up with more plasticine.

Make your own Christmas calendar with a surprise in it for each day. You need twenty-four small patch pockets on a piece of material. Choose a piece for the backing about the size of a tea towel, the pockets can be made from scraps as they are quite small. Stitch the pockets round three sides and put a tiny present – a sweet or a small toy – in each. Hang the top over a wire clothes hanger, and take out a present each day in December.

Another decoration for Christmas or Hallowe'en is an Apple Man. Draw a face on a walnut and stick it to a big apple with sticky tape. Glue on some pieces of cotton wool for a beard and hair, and make a pointed hat out of paper. Cut a pipe cleaner into half and stick on each piece for arms (use sticky tape again). Make a small cloak out of crêpe paper, just long enough to cover the sticky tape. Make the arms hold a twig broom. At Christmas he can sweep up salt snow. At Hallowe'en he can sweep up tiny bits of leaves.

If you want a change from holly or paper chains make some rose garlands. Cut crêpe paper pieces into the shape of a pointed spear end, leaving a bit to hold on to underneath. Gently pull the centre of the paper so it stretches and you have a petal ready to curl round other petals. Carry on until you have made a satisfactory rose then secure the ends with thin wire or wool. Tie a number of roses on to string with a few green leaves and hang up.

I, said the donkey all shaggy and brown,
I, carried his mother up-hill and down,
I, carried her safely to Bethlehem town,
I, said the donkey all shaggy and brown.

I, said the ox all white and red,
I, gave him my hay to pillow his head,
I, gave him my hay to make his bed,
I, said the ox, all white and red.

I, said the sheep with the curly horns
I, gave him my wool to keep him warm,
I, gave my coat on Christmas morn,
I, said the sheep with the curly horns.

I, said the dove from the rafters high,
I, cooed him to sleep so he would not cry,
Cooed him to sleep, my mate and I
I, said the dove from the rafters high.

Thus every beast, every bird as well,
In the stable there was wont to tell
Of the gift he gave Emmanuel,
Of the gift he gave Emmanuel.

Christmas is coming
The goose is getting fat
Please put a penny
In the old man's hat.

Instead of glass balls to hang on Christmas trees, what about ping pong balls? Draw a face, then glue on a cotton wool beard. Glue some crêpe paper round the top for a hat and gather this with thin thread which can then be hung on to the tree. Another idea is to stick thread to a ping pong ball, cover it in liquid glue then roll it in some glitter. You could even add a bit of hanging tinsel.

You could help tidy up by this hat game for Christmas morning or after parties. Put a tall paper hat on your head and have screwed-up bits of paper thrown into it. Try to keep the bits in your hat while trying to throw bits into somebody else's hat.

When you've got a store of bits, play the carrier bag game. Stand a fair distance away from the bag and throw all bits into it.

When you've got only one bit of screwed-up paper left set up a mini golf course. Make a tunnel out of boxes or a book, and narrow lanes out of pieces of string. Now, with a roll of newspaper, hit the paper round the course. Play by yourself or take turns with somebody else.

Legs are very useful things
They keep your tummy off the floor
And when you want to leave the room
They walk you through the door.

Legs are very useful things
They help you carry round your head
And when your face is feeling tired
They carry it to bed.

Index

Ideas that can start from having some of the following:

Ideas for the child alone

Ideas for two or more

Other Books and Records

From Play School

Play School Play Ideas, Ruth Craft
Humpty's Rhymes
Storytime from Play School, (published jointly with Pan Books)
More Stories from Play School, (published jointly with Pan Books)

From Play School and Play Away

The Bold Bad Bus and other Rhymes, Wilma Horsbrugh
Bang on a Drum – Songs from Play School and Play Away, (published jointly with Keith Prowse Music Group)

Records

Play School (stories) RBT 10
Sing a Song of Play School REC 212
The Tale of a Donkey's Tail and Other Stories REC 232
Bang on a Drum REC 242

Also available in Cassette